Fundamentals of English Grammar

By

Dr. Noah

Grammar is a piano I play by ear. All I know about grammar is its power.

Copyright

Dr. Noah

I think most people agree there is a component of skill in art making; you have to learn grammar before you learn how to write.

What is Grammar?

Grammar is a system of rules and principles for speaking and writing a language.

It's perfectly obvious that there is some genetic factor that distinguishes humans from other animals and that it is language-specific. The theory of that genetic component, whatever it turns out to be, is what is called universal grammar.

I taught myself algebra and a little grammar, and somehow I scraped a high enough score on the ACT to be admitted to Brigham Young University, even though I had no formal education.

I've always felt like I could express myself better in English just because the way the grammar works.

Grammar is the set of structural rules governing the composition of clauses, phrases, and words in a given language.

Speakers of any language have a set of rules for using that language, and these rules forms that language's grammar.

The majority of the information in the grammar is acquired not by conscious study or instruction, but by observing other speakers. Much of this work is done during childhood;

Learning any language later in life often involves a greater degree of explicit instruction. Thus, grammar is the cognitive information underlying language use.

The term "grammar" also describes the rules that govern the linguistic behavior of a group of speakers. The term "English grammar", then may have many meanings. Grammar may refer to the whole of English grammar, that is, to the grammars of all the speakers of the language, in which case, the term covers a great deal of variation.

Grammar can also refer to what is common to the grammars of all, or of the vast majority of English speakers. Or it may refer to the rules of a particular, relatively well-defined variety of English (such as some Standard English for a particular region).

Your grammar is a reflection of your image. Good or bad, you have made an impression. And like all impressions, you are in total control.

Writing is an act of faith, not a trick of grammar.

Like everything metaphysical the harmony between thought and reality is to be found in the grammar of the language.

Table of Contents

I. The Sentence and its Parts, page 11

II. Words and Their Uses, page 39

If you want to know the way to my heart... good spelling and good grammar, good punctuation, capitalize only where you are supposed to capitalize, it's done.

Because there is no better tool for writing than experience. It has very little to do with grammar and everything to do with knowing.

The Sentence and its Parts

0. Sentence

A sentence is a group of words expressing a complete thought. A sentence contains a **Subject** and a **Predicate**.

1. Parts of a Sentence
There are several elements or parts that may be in a sentence. They are:
a. **Subject**
b. **Predicate**
c. **Complement**
d. **Phrase**
e. **Modifier**
f. **Clause**

The two <u>necessary</u> parts of a sentence are the **subject** and the **predicate**.

Example 1:

She left. (Subject, Predicate only)

Example 2:

Go. (**You** is the subject of the verb **go**)

2. Subject

The subject of a sentence is that part about which something is being said. The subject is the doer of the action.

Example 1:

Noah ran to the market.

Example 2:

The little **dog** fell into the hole.

3. Simple Subject

The simple subject is the particular word or words about which something is being said. Modifiers are not part of it.

Examples:

That brown **book** is worth twenty dollars.

His famous **Frankenstein** was a best seller.

Abraham Lincoln was the sixteenth President.

4. Complete Subject

The complete subject is the simple subject with all its modifiers.

Examples:

That brown book is worth twenty dollars.

His famous Frankenstein was a best seller.

Abraham Lincoln was the sixteenth President.

5. Compound Subject

A compound subject is a subject that consists of two or more words connected usually by **or**, or **and**.

Examples:
Noah and **Mary** were there.

(**Noah** and **Mary** make up the compound subject)

Wheat, **rye**, **oats**, or **corn** were needed.

- Throughout this study guide, **subject** refers only to simple subject.

6. Predicate

The predicate is that part which **says something** about the subject. The predicate expresses the action of the sentence. It tells what is being done.

Examples:

Noah **ran** to the market.

The little dog **fell** into the hole.

7. Simple Predicate

The simple predicate is the particular word or words that express the action. Modifiers are not part of the simple predicate. The simple predicate is the verb.

Examples:

I **read** this book last year.

Noah **was going** to the market.

8. Complete Predicate

The complete predicate is the simple predicate with all its modifiers.

Examples:

I **read this book last year**.

Noah **was going to the market**.

9. Compound Predicate

The compound predicate is a predicate which consists of two or more verbs that are usually connected by **and**.

Examples:

Noah **ran** the relay and **threw** the javelin.

She **reads**, **writes**, and **speaks** Spanish fluently.

10. Complement

The complement is a word that completes the meaning or action of the predicate. There are several types:

1. objects
   a. direct objects
   b. indirect objects

2. subject complements
   a. predicate nominatives (something divided into predicate nous and predicate pronoun).
   b. predicate adjectives

11. Object

An object is a complement that completes the action of transitive verbs. An object never follows a linking or intransitive verb.

Examples:

She used the **car** last.

He gave **her** the **list**.

12. Direct Object

The direct object of a verb receivers the action of the verb or shows the result of the action. It answers the question **What**? Or **Whom**? After an action verb.

She used the **car** last.

(She used **What**? car)

Mary liked **him** very much.

(Mary liked **Whom**? him)

13. Indirect Object

The indirect object of a verb precedes the direct object. It usually tells **for whom** or **to whom** the action of the verb is done.

There can be direct object without an indirect object, but there cannot be an indirect object without a direct object.

Indirect objects are usually found with verbs like **bought**, **gave**, **took**, **offer**, **showed**, etc.

He gave **Marry** the pen.
The tutor showed **him** his grade.

14. Subject Complement

A subject complement is a complement that refers back to the subject. It follows linking verbs. It never follows transitive or action verbs. Two kinds of subject complements are the **predicate adjective** and the **predicate nominative**.

15. Predicate Adjective

A predicate adjective is an adjective that follows a linking verb and modifies the subject for the sentence.

Examples:

The ocean was dark **blue**.

She is **famous** for her cooking.

16. Predicate Nominative

A predicate nominative is a noun or pronoun which refers back to the subject and can usually be interchanged with it. A predicate nominative follows a linking verbs.

Examples:

Noah and Marry were the **winners**. (Noah and Marry = winners. The winners were Noah and Marry.)

It was **he** who won.

17. Phrase

A phrase is a group of related words not expressing a complete thought and without a subject and predicate. A phrase is a part of a sentence. There are **verbal** and **prepositional** phrases.

18. Prepositional Phrase

A prepositional phrase is a phrase starting with a preposition and is used to modify the other words.

Examples:

He stepped to **the edge of the river**.

For two hours they waited **in the cold**.

19. Kinds of Prepositional Phrases

The two kinds of prepositional phrases are **adverb** and **adjective**.

20. Adverb phrase

An adverbial prepositional phrase is one that modifies a verb, an adjective, or an adverb. When modifying a verb, it tells **how**, **when**, **where**, or **why**.

Examples:

The basketball fell **though the net**.

The wall was light blue **with a light border**.

The bus arrived late **in the afternoon**.

21. Adjective Phrase

An adjective prepositional phrase is one that modifies a noun or a pronoun.

Examples:

The pocket of **the shirt** was torn.

She helped the bird **with a broken wing**.

22. Verbal Phrase

A verbal phrase is a phrase introduced by a verbal.

The three kinds of verbal phrases are participle phrase, gerund phrase, and infinitive phrase.

Examples:

The pocket of **the shirt** was torn.

She helped the bird **with a broken wing**.

23. Participial Phrase

A participial phrase is a phrase starting with a participle. The phrase includes the participle and its modifiers and complement. A participial phrase is used like an adjective.

Examples:

They watched the workers **building the house**.

Being wrong most of the time, she lost confidence.

24. Gerund Phrase

A gerund phrase is a phrase starting with a gerund and its modifiers and complement. Gerund phrases are used like nouns.

Examples:

Earning the award was very difficult. (The phrase is the subject of the sentence).

For **playing music** she was fired. (The phrase is the object of the preposition **for**).

The thing that's depressing is teaching graduate students today and discovering that they don't know simple elemental facts of grammar. They really do not know how to scan a line; they've never been taught to scan a line. Many of them don't know the difference between 'lie' and 'lay,' let alone 'its' and 'it's.' And they're in graduate school!

25. Infinitive Phrase

An infinitive phrase is a phrase introduced by an infinitive. An infinitive phrase is made up of the infinitive and its modifiers and complement. It may be used as a nun, an adjective, or an adverb.

To refuse the invitation seemed bad. (Infinitive phrase is used as a noun as the subject.)

Shakespeare's work is a book to read slowly. (The infinitive phrase is used as an adjective modifying **book**.)

He listened carefully **to hear the song**. (The infinitive phrase is used as an adverb modifying the vey **listened**.)

Encourage children to write their own stories, and then don't rain on their parade. Don't say, 'That's not true.' Applaud flights of fantasy. Help with spelling and grammar, but stand up and cheer the use of imagination.

Words and their uses

The eight ways in which words are used are called eight parts of speech. The eight classifications are **noun, pronoun, adjective, verb, adverb, preposition, interjection**, and **conjunction**.

Some words called homographs can be used in a sentence before one can determine their use.

1. A **noun** is the name of anything.
2. A **pronoun** takes the place of a noun.
3. A **verb** expresses action or state of being.
4. An **adjective** modifies a noun or a pronoun.

5. An **adverb** modifies a verb, an adjective, or another adverb.
6. A **preposition** shows a relationship between its object and another word in the sentence.
7. An **interjection** expresses strong feeling.
8. A **conjunction** connects words, phrases, and clauses.

I had really good English teachers in elementary through high school. Not only were we required to read a lot - which is the best training for writing - we were drilled on grammar every day, every night. I hated the drill part, but I don't dangle my participles too often.